ANISHINAABE
SONGS FOR
A NEW
MILLENNIUM

ANISHINAABE

SONGS FOR

A NEW

MILLENNIUM

MARCIE R. RENDON

UNIVERSITY OF MINNESOTA PRESS

MINNEAPOLIS LONDON

Photographs by Cheryl Walsh Bellville. www.cwbphotography.com

Publication History on pages 65–67 gives original publication and performance information for the poems and songs compiled in this book.

For information about musical performances of "Of This Turtle Isle," "Spring Wind Dances at the River," "Thunder Calling," or "Buffalo Woman," contact Brent Michael Davids–Blue Butterfly Group, filmcomposer.us. For information about musical performances of "Dakota Land," "Thunder Woman," or "Grandmother Walks," contact Ann Millikan, Sword Dance Publishing Company, www.annmillikan.com.

Published by the University of Minnesota Press
111 Third Avenue South, Suite 290
Minneapolis, MN 55401-2520
http://www.upress.umn.edu

ISBN 978-1-5179-1743-2 (pb)

Library of Congress record available at https://lccn.loc.gov/2024007582

Printed in the United States of America on acid-free paper

The University of Minnesota is an equal-opportunity educator and employer.

32 31 30 29 28 27 26 25 24   10 9 8 7 6 5 4 3 2 1

to those who have gone before; to those who are yet to come
to those who are ever present who sing their songs for us to hear

CONTENTS

AUTHOR'S NOTE

The ancestors who walk with us sing us our song. When we get
quiet enough, we can hear them sing and make them audible
to people today. We still exist. Our ancestors exist. Our songs
exist. Anishinaabe have not stopped creating songs for our
people. This is a collection of my Anishinaabe songs for the new
millennium.

While I am not able to write in Ojibwemowin, the language
of my mother and grandparents, some of my poetic writing
style is consistent with the ancient songs of my people—short,
descriptive "poem songs" or "dream songs." The ancient dream
songs were recorded in pictographs on birchbark scrolls; my
poem–dream songs for the new millennium are written in
English and inscribed on paper.

One of the major influences on my writing was the book
Summer in the Spring: Anishinaabe Lyric Poems and Stories, edited
and interpreted by Ojibwe author Gerald Vizenor and published
by the University of Oklahoma Press in 1963, with later editions
in 1979, 1981, and 1993. This book validated my own writing
style and encouraged me to continue to write short verse in the
style of my ancestors. Vizenor wrote, "The Anishinaabe heard
stories in their dream songs. Tribal visions were natural sources
of intuition and identities, and some tribal visions were spiritual
transmigrations that inspired the lost and lonesome souls of the
woodland to be healed."

Prior to contact, Anishinaabe people have a centuries-long
history of composing song in the Ojibwe language without

written word. The stories and songs were passed down generationally through memorization, with a cultural agreement to not "steal" another's poem songs. In this way, through oral tradition and pictograph, the poem songs in Vizenor's book were available to him to be translated and written down. My writing of these dream song–poems validates for me that our ways of life and of seeing the world are not lost; rather, we, as writers and visionaries, can carry the practice of dream songs forward to and for new generations.

I have also had opportunities to write lyrics for theatrical productions, choral numbers, and operas. Some of these songs are also included here. The lyrics have been set to musical notation by professional musicians I have had the honor to work with. Creating song. Creating beauty. Another way for our stories to be heard.

Because of removal, dislocation, assimilation, and acculturation many of us have been led to believe that the old ways are lost. While it is important to learn our language and attend our ceremonies, we must also allow ourselves to be quiet enough to hear the spirits who are always with us. They will talk to us. They will teach us. They will heal us. They will sing our song to us.

I

DREAM SONGS

thunder calling
I heard that bird
sitting on the ground

gentle moonbeams
blossom on
the windowsill

1. grandmother walks moonlit trails
sucking maple syrup cubes
birchbark wraps itself around her
while black bear guards her path

2. at the water's edge
in a rock upon the path
flickering in an evening flame
I see her face

3. mist rises off the lake
trees shiver
fish slide
spirits rise
ancestors sing
away
aloneness

4. grandmother stands on sacred ground
the ancient ways are never lost
only,
maybe,
      temporarily forgotten
        lakes of rice
        and turtle island riverbeds
        regenerate ancestral memory
          it is not a gift easily forgotten
I remember my ancestors' words

1. I lie on the bones of my ancestors
rhythms of silence run deep

as each breath

each breath gives life

2. our grandmothers' dust
is watered with the fallen dreams
of all women
all women
              all women
sacrifice dreams for future generations

3. a breath of wind
weaves water
weaving dreams
we live whole lives between
each breath

4. our grandmothers' dust
waters our dreams
this accumulation of hope
feeds our souls
              women
breathe life
breathe life into being

5. in this season of abundance
hear grandmother's breath echo
her breath moves
all the winds of time
all life intertwined

6. earth memory holds me
holds me to the ground
holds me on the ground
holds me in the ground
and sets me free

from a beaded leather bag tied around her waist
she feeds me popped mahnomen
    in the crook of a cottonwood tree
    winter breeze shakes crystal prisms to the ground
she feeds my spirit hope on ice sharpened days and nights

singing songs ahead
to future generations
creating visions
of the world we want to see
so that on their day of
hearing
they will know we
sat
and in the quiet of our minds
sang a song of beauty forward
and dreamt a
loving day

I go to sleep to dream
coming awake
to live

creator
you are here next to me
    all my thoughts
       and dreams
are prayers to you

trusting in
your strength

to guide me through
this life
they call reality

I pray for dreams
direction
guidance

loneliness for voices, faces

have I forgotten to honor your presence
caught up in day to day living

I pray for dreams

I saw the stars
reflected in the water
a motionless mirror
of the full moon sky

earth roots are the hardest
    to keep growing

1. water ripples
    life
    swells into being

2. sister
I have heard you sing of water
give each birth
the strength of your songs
    as grandmother moon
    gives you her strength
    in your sleepless dreams

3. water
    held back
    by
    earth
weathering away resistance
    persistent
    life giver
flowing waves
ease the fear
and fill
    with awe

4. children
you had a name
from where you came
they know you where you are going
from the future
they gently call your name

you think I do nothing
all day
I am busy loving
human beings

women sing
and
spirit light travels
back to ancient
peoples
and
forward
to all the
future generations

woman, you are
strength
you have given birth
to daytime visions
and nighttime dreams
you are
the keeper
of a nation
yet to be born

there is no sorrow
no death
only the empty hollow of what could have been
    negative shadow images aren't any less a picture

while grandchildren sleep
the songs of elders rise from the homeland
and children waiting to be born sing ancestral victory songs

as I hear their songs, I sit
in this gentle moment of snow melt
while the smells of spring
and hope of summer
rise from the moistened earth,
green buds, cold this morning,
hold the promise of singing cottonwood leaves
in the summer wind

love wraps around the roots of trees
intertwines and turns and twirls
love wraps around the roots of trees
growing into moistened soil
out into the rising sun
    god meant for us to rise from darkness
    burst full flame unto the earth
    wrap around
    entwine our love
reach out to those who hunger
thirst with stunted growth
nothing
no one can stop the moving
of love entwined
as it bursts full flame upon the earth

1. call the winds of healing
sing your grief into being

2. call the winds of grief
sing your healing into being

3. tears are raindrops
that cleanse the soul

dreams wash spirits
in midnight waters
migratory journeys heal
what was never really broken

hold the night sky close
    wrap your body in its silken softness
    and cry the morning dew

The wind catches my songs
Carried on strands of memory
Children
Hear me sing

Our ancestors dreamt your future
The iron rail, Angus cows slumbering in shorn prairie
The buffalo remembered only on the metal
That buys and sells on the grain exchange

There are those moments at the Mississippi when a breeze
Through the ancient cottonwoods remembers
The absent sound of well-worn leather moccasins
And the silent slide of birchbark on muddy water
The moments when even you feel memory rise on neck hairs

Our ancestors dreamt your future
While writing our future on wiigwaasabak; petroglyphs
The Midewinini secured our future in limestone caves

the earth shakes
shifts priorities
winds cleanse
snow protects
rain nurtures
those who think
the earth has gone
crazy
just don't understand
a mother's instincts

ancestors travel
    riding shotgun
    for wayward granddaughters
to distant shores
they travel
for the first time
tasting salt water
and touch bark
of trees that aren't
birch or pine
    see flowers during
    our winter
    and
    walk on desert dust
these travels
carry their
dreams forward

1. I am a seemingly silent river
hold me close
and you will feel
the rapids
raging

2. you may dam the river
but can you still the tide?

1. a turquoise aura filled the air around her
holding close
with supple willow arms
  she sang in gentle murmurs while
  cottonwood leaves slip-slapped against each other
  in the cool summer breeze
    gently
    she rocked my soul
    holding it out of harm's way
ash-gray hair fanned my cheeks
while breathing life into
childhood dreams
  with hope I held on fast, arms wrapped around her waist,
through tornado winds
she dreamed a future into being

2. she walks the other side
midnight dreams
a dim reflection
of a lifetime of living

3. dreams
are visions
of a life to be
clarity offered in the
haze of their
unreality

4. ancient secrets
reveal
spirits washed in midnight waters
migratory journeys are taken
to heal what was never really broken

eagle dancers
dreamt to me
shimmery whiteness
travels
from this life
to a truer reality

I have heard some of
our people say
"I am tired of eagles and pipes
there is more to being indian today
than ghosts of the past"

eagle dancers
dreamt to me
as I hold this sacred feather
the smallness of me
the eternity of you

I am tired too
let me dream
of eagle dancers
traveling
on shimmery whiteness
from this life
to a truer reality

1. This desert is a sea of sorrow
Blood coagulates
Dries before it can offer life

2. Chik chak
Clak clik
Chik chak
    Baby bones
Sun bleached
Dried
Chik chak

3. Sinewed dreams string together bones of hope
Scattered through the grains of sand
Birds pick life clean, get fat on dropped dreams
Bones strung together with dried, sinewed dreams

4. In this graveyard of dreams
Rattlesnake poison bleaches bones
On a constant day of dead
Bones speak of lost family, forests green, moisture rich tropical
    days and nights
Forgotten prayers drop like rain
An altar forms from east to west
A constant day of dead

1. I am the soul of all the ancient warriors
born of the desert when
no concrete or metal wall
stopped the light of the sun
or outshone the moon
I am no boundaries
I am ancient dreams
foretelling
global warming
I am the sharp pain of reality

2. I am the soul of all the ancient warriors
born of the desert
I am the blinding mirror image
of near-sighted dreams
I am no boundaries
try stop me
I go where I want
I am the nightmare
of short-sighted vision
foretelling
no water
strip-mined mountains
scorching heat
I am the sharp pain of
overheated global reality

dropping seeds
for next year's beauty
water flows
flower grows
pain erased with nature's healing

what if I never said another thing
but sat silently
    smoking filterless cigarettes
    drinking columbian coffee
holding grandchild after grandchild
on a lap ever softer, ever bonier with age

what if I never wrote another word
but filled my heart with beauty
    sat silently wrapped in fog
    while thunderstorms shook me to the bones
    and lightning currents
    connected brainwave/thought waves
    to spirits dancing on the shoreline
would my silence drive you crazy

II

PERFORMANCE
SONGS

WHITE MAN'S MUSIC

white man's music
doesn't feed the soul
metal strings sound across square walls restraining passion
men and women, too afraid to meet
dance on cold tile floors
    broad feet encased, encumbered
    in leather-bound souls, laces pulled too tight

let me dance across water-swollen prairie,
    ankle-deep in spring mud
as migrants in the field
yearn for just one more guitar string
singing songs of being
foreigners on their own homeland

JACK'S 49

I don't care who you love
    I can find another one
    Leech Lake, Red Lake
    Mdewakanton Sioux
    I can snag a rich one too

I don't care who you love
    I can find another one
    Pine Ridge, Rosebud
    Fond du lac
    I can snag a poor one too

MADDOG & OGICHIDAG

Maddog:
    Loneliness and maddog
    My constant company
    Twelve years of mission school
    Erased my history
    Loneliness and maddog
    My only company

Ogichidag:
    Wake up old man
    Have a memory

Maddog:
    Loneliness
    Confusion
    Delusional
    Illusions
    All I have are
    Drunken bones
    A logger's
    Long forgotten dreams
    Loneliness and maddog
    To keep me
    Company

Ogichidag:
    Wake up
    Old man
    There are no
    Broken memories
    Only
    Forgotten destinies

Maddog:
    Oh wa Ya hey
    Oh wa hey
    Drunken dreams
    Are all you get from me
    You want
    To know
    The past
    My son

    (pause)

    Oh wa Ya hey
    Oh wa
    Hey
    Romantic inconsideration
    For a history
    Drenched in blood
    Relocation
    Forced
    Acculturation
    Termination
    Ex
    Communication
    Ahm-ni–o
    Dohm-ni-o
    Jesus christ *(laughs)*

    Oh wa Ya hey
    Oh wa
    Hey
    Romantic inconsideration
    For a history

Drenched in blood
Maddog and loneliness
My only company

Ogichidag:

I offered you tobacco
You pocketed the same
All I'm asking old man
Is to give me
a name

Maddog:

Maddog
Reddog
Jackpine
Tree
Winter winds
Snowblind
Old fools like me

Ogichidag:

Wake up
Old man
There are no
Broken memories
Only
Forgotten destinies

Maddog:

Blackdog
Old dog
Crow dog
Spotted hawk

Three
Yellow hawk
Raven wing
Goddamn me

Ogichidag:
There are no
Broken memories
Only forgotten destinies

Maddog:
The trees
They speak to me

Ogichidag:
The jackpine and the cedar
Preserve a dreamer's memory

Maddog:
The trees
They speak to me

Ogichidag:
Birch and willow
Hold dreams
Waiting to be free

Maddog:
Maddog
Drunkdog
Gi-chi-guy-ay
Oh wa hey
Reddog

Yellow dog
Jackpine
Tree
Dreams
Set free
Maddog
Blackdog
Gitch-ee-guy-ya
Maddog

(pause)

Gitch-gi-dag
o-gitch-gi-dag—aye
o-gitch-gi-dag—aye
o-gitch-gi-dag
o-gitch-gi-dag—aye

Maddog & Ogichidag:
Drunken bones
And long forgotten dreams
Remembered destiny
The jackpine and the cedar
Preserve a dreamer's memory

SONG OF THE SOUL

At the dawn of my awakening
I cross the veil of sorrow
Fearing, nevermore, will I hear angels sing

I walk into shadow
Sorrow holds me in its grasp

I see into the world
A child's ghetto eyes, devoid of destiny

In a flash of clarity
I see into the mirror of celestial memory

And understand god's plan for me

At the dawn of my awakening
god reaps a field of hope
The only promise for tomorrow
Are the dreams I sing today

    Sun-drenched wheat fields
    Healing rays of god's love
    Wash gently over me

    Sun-drenched wheat fields
    All my sorrow heals
    god in all her wonder
    Plants songs in souls like me
    My summer soul is fertile
    With dreams waiting to sing free

OF THIS TURTLE ISLE

una gente en Dios
a people in God
in God
en Dios
Indians

on a ship bound from nowhere
we land on turtle isle

in the shadow of the morning
    in the hands of innocence
a wild child
ghetto child
    walks me safely home
lost on a foreign continent
no place to call my own

in the concrete village
far from saigon
in a steel glass jungle
    a wild child
    rez child
        walks me safely home
lost on a foreign continent
no place to call my own

on turtle isle
compassion frees my soul
elders hold our language to our ear
while our children ghetto speak

with ageless innocence
their bodies move to the heartbeat
of this turtle isle

When writing "Of This Turtle Isle," I thought about the Phillips neighborhood in Minneapolis and how it is the gathering place for newly landed immigrants, how this land is historically Native land, and how my ancestors (Indigenous people) welcomed new peoples to this continent until such time as we were brutalized. I thought about how Columbus described the Indigenous people he first saw as "children of God," which may be where the term "Indians" really came from, "en Dios." I thought about how we still welcome people to this continent, no matter how impoverished we are and how most groups, including those who have been here for generations, don't seem to recognize that we still exist. Yet the spirits of our ancestors hold out that the Indigenous people of the world will lead the rest of humanity to a more human reality. Our children, no matter how confusing it gets in the material world, are still spoken to by spirit, often through our elders. This "continental" community can survive only by adhering to, listening to, the voices of the ancestors and by being one with Turtle Island.

—M. R.

DAKOTA LAND

Haha Wakpa
Misizibi
Wakan Tipi stone hollow.
From the cave
Wakan Tipi,
edge of the world
Dakota walk into the known,
lives watered by Haha Wakpa.

Moccasins
mold to rock on trail,
bluffs to
mighty river
Haha Wakpa.

Underground springs feed cottonwood,
giving birth to Dakota.
Cottonwood speaks,
wind whirling over the hollow
singing Dakota songs.

Han, mitakuyepi
All my relations.
Han, mitakuyepi
All my relations.

SPRING WIND DANCES AT THE RIVER

MINNESOTA

Little Crow, Little Crow, 1862
Ta-hey-tan Wa-ka-wa Mee-nee, 1862
Oak scaffolding, platform, and skeleton,
Sing a Dakota death song.

Maple tree and cottonwood leaves
Drop into the river like tears,
Crying a nation's secret shame.
Until today, until today.

Immigrant settlers grieve,
A thousand of their own lost,
Until today on rolling farmland.
Until today, until today.

Today, when winters freeze the muddy banks,
Barren trees hang with arctic ice.
Dakota death songs, warrior songs,
Breathe on the icy wind.

A Victory Song snaps the cold;
The river floods, washing mother earth.
Rivers flood, leaving medicine
Rooted in spring-warmed soil.

Zi-gwan No-din Nee-mee Zee-bee
Spring Wind Dances at the River.
Zi-gwan No-din Nee-mee Zee-bee
Spring Wind Dances at the River.

SAINTE CROIX

Springtime water swirls in eddies.
White shining river, currents washing
Tree roots lined along the river bank,
White swirling wampum.

Catfish stalking the estuary
Carry hopes and dreams to
Promenading corn, beans, and squash,
Three sisters waving along the shore.

A river people with twin white names:
Saint Francis's Indians, *Natio Luporem,*
Nation of Wolves;
Wa-bum Ah-kee, WA-be-na-kee,
Ah-be-na-kee, White Dawn Nation,
People living at the white sunrise.

Mounds of sisters, mounds of people.
Earthen mounds inhabit the banks.
Mounds of sisters, mounds of people
Carry hopes and dreams to future generations.

Zi-gwan No-din Nee-mee Zee-bee
Spring Wind Dances at the River.
Zi-gwan No-din Nee-mee Zee-bee
Spring Wind Dances at the River.

MISSISSIPPI

Glacial aquifers store
the embryo of our forebears.
Gi chi Zee bee history flowing,
Vaulting forward, running;
An ice box autobiography.

Ancient memories revolt, melting,
Push up, ascending to the surface.
Ancestors leap and come to life.
Legends mingle, spit, and harmonize.

Warriors skulk along the shores,
Round dance, two-step and cut loose!
Belt out songs of sport and battles;
Win or lose, there's dancing to be done.

Young and callow is the old man river,
Rolling carefree with no affiliation.
But Wise Old Woman Spirit sings of hope;
She plants her dream in every generation.

Old Woman Spirit sings for balance and hope;
She plants her dream in every generation.
Old Woman Spirit sings for balance and hope;
She plants her dream in every generation.

Zi-gwan No-din Nee-mee Zee-bee
Spring Wind Dances at the River.
Zi-gwan No-din Nee-mee Zee-bee
Spring Wind Dances at the River.

SING THE SPIRIT HOME

Sing the spirit home
Dance the spirit home

>   The elders say
>   There is no beginning
>   There is no end
> All of life a circle

Birth is the coming of the spirit to this world
Death is the going of the spirit to that world
All of life a circle
>   Sing the spirit home
>   Dance the spirit home

You, my child, have traveled Jiibay Ziibi
>   Back and forth
Across the rainbow of the universe
>   Grandmother's hands gather spirit
>   Grandmother's hands guide you home
Bringing old/new life home
Walking, dancing through universal timelessness
Grandmother guides you home

Some are finished with their eternal journey
Others
>   Return and return

Sing the Spirit home
Dance the Spirit home
ancestral memories, ancestral teachings
embedded in our tribal consciousness

THUNDER CALLING

Thunder calling,
With no compassion,
A nation wages war.
Blood red lake water
Chills the souls of innocence,
As a people die.

Thunder calling,
Water beings swim to shore
A nation needs to heal.
Blue lightning bolts flash death across the sky.
Native nations cannot die.

Thunder calling,
In secret caves, on stone walls,
Elders paint images of peace,
A permanent agreement
Made with spirits of the underworld.
Native nations will not die.

Thunder calling,
Thunder people carry bones,
Souls and bones of dear departed.
Grief makes the journey eons long.
All the people of a nation cry.
We cannot die.

Thunder calling,
Bear stomps the earth.
Thunder calling,
Bear, ya he ya.

Bear stomps a healing song.
Healing all the nations gathered,
Intertwined in ancient healing.
Relatives and enemies lay down weapons all.
Native nations will not die.

Buried in the prairie earth,
Ancient spirits heal
All the people's rage and sorrow.

BUFFALO WOMAN

she's a buffalo woman giving birth to a thunder nation
she's a buffalo woman giving birth to a thunder nation
she's a buffalo woman giving birth to a thunder nation
she's a buffalo woman giving birth to a thunder nation

>   strawberries if you're hungry
>   blueberries hold the sky
>   earth in all her glory
>   feeds both you, you and i

she's a buffalo woman giving birth to a thunder nation
she's a buffalo woman giving birth to a thunder nation
she's a buffalo woman giving birth to a thunder nation
she's a buffalo woman giving birth to a thunder nation

>   strawberries if you're hungry
>   blueberries hold the sky
>   earth in all her glory
>   feeds both you, you and i

she's a buffalo woman giving birth to a thunder nation
she's a buffalo woman giving birth to a thunder nation

THUNDER WOMAN (LIGHTNESS INTO DARK)

lightness
into
dark
darkness
into
light

she danced
across the arctic sky
danced darkness
into
light
lightness
into
dark
the
midnight sun
called her name
she danced

midnight darkness
fed her soul
she danced
her image into being
sapphire
emerald
ruby
opal

from the caverns of the earth
she danced

mirrored prisms
she danced
the darkness
into
being

she soared
the day
into being
soaring
higher
higher
leading sun
out of dawn
into being
she soared
east to west
and back around
leading sun
she chased the midnight
out of dawn

she rumbled
waddled
sleek and sure
past the sagebrush
tiny seeds
caught in
massive paws
eating
berries
farther north
the seeds are dropped

she rumbled
waddled
sleek and sure
past tobacco leaves
seeds carried
north
in shaggy fur
she rumbled
waddled
with the healing
healing earth
as farther north
she goes

she stomped
stomped
herself
into being

striking fast
and leaving slow
she burst upon the prairie

heard them call her name
thunder
Thunder
Thunder Woman
she heard them
call her name
she stomped herself
into being
destruction reigns
and

lightning
heals
she stomped across
the sky

sun &
moon &
stars
go running
she stomps herself
into being

ACKNOWLEDGMENTS

Miigwech to the elders who have guided, taught, and protected me throughout my life.

Thank you to Franconia Sculpture Garden Writing Residency for the time and space to gather my thoughts to put this manuscript together.

Thanks to Jacqui Lipton, my agent, and to Erik Anderson, my editor.

Thanks to Cheryl Walsh Bellville for the beautiful photographs and the years of support prior to this book reaching fruition.

Thanks to all the drum groups I've listened to, and to classical composers Brent Michael Davids (Mohican/Munsee-Lenape) and Ann Millikan for saying, "Oh, of course you can write a song."

Any misspelling of Ojibwe is on me. We can be gentle with each other as we learn.

PUBLICATION HISTORY

Previous versions of the poems in this book were published in the following publications or performed at the following events.

"thunder calling" commissioned by The Festival Choir of Madison (2006). Music by Brent Michael Davids.

"grandmother walks . . . mist rises . . . grandmother stands" from *Traces in Blood, Bone, and Stone: Contemporary Ojibwe Poetry,* edited by Kimberly Blaeser (Bemidji, Minn.: Loonfeather Press, 2006).

"children / you had a name" from the author's play *Bring the Children Home* (1996).

"earth memory holds me" from https://indigenousvoices .blogspot.com/.

"singing songs ahead" from *Yellow Medicine Review* (2021).

"woman, you are" from *Fireweed: A Feminist Quarterly,* edited by Ivy Chaske and Connie Fife, Toronto, Canada (Winter 1986).

"while grandchildren sleep" from *Yellow Medicine Review* (2014).

"Our ancestors dreamt your future" from *St. Paul Almanac,* Impressions Project (2017).

"I am a seemingly silent river" from *Speaking in Tongues,* anthology of the Loft Inroads Program (1994).

"This desert is a sea of sorrow" from *Yellow Medicine Review,* edited by Steven Pacheco (Spring 2012).

"I am the soul of all the ancient warriors" from *Yellow Medicine Review,* edited by Steven Pacheco (Spring 2012).

"Spirit Woman" from the author's play *SongCatcher* (1998).

"Jack's 49" from the author's play *SongCatcher* (1998).

"Maddog & Ogichidag," duet written at Nautilus Music-Theater Composer–Librettist Studio (2000).

"Song of the Soul" written at Nautilus Music-Theater Composer–Librettist Studio (2000).

"Dakota Land" written for Ann Millikan's opera *Swede Hollow* (2012). http://www.annmillikan.com.

"Of This Turtle Isle" commissioned by World Voices (2001). Artistic director Karle Erickson. Music by Brent Michael Davids.

"Spring Wind Dances at the River" commissioned to commemorate the Mingling of Waters Ceremony of the Grand Excursion Celebration, July 4, 2004. Music by Brent Michael Davids.

"Sing the Spirit Home" written in response to *"those that have gone before us and all those yet unborn,"* AICHO art show, Duluth. Painting by Sylvia Houle (2022).

"Buffalo Woman" written at Nautilus Music-Theater Composer–Librettist Studio (2000). Music by Brent Michael Davids.

"Thunder Woman (Lightness into Dark)" for the Manitou Project, composer Ann Millikan (2011). Honorable mention in poetry contest of American Association of University Women (1992). Nitaawichige, Poetry Harbor (2002). First published in *Rising Dawn,* Archdiocese of St. Paul/Minneapolis (Fall 1998).

Marcie R. Rendon (White Earth Ojibwe) is a poet, mystery writer, and playwright in Minneapolis. She received Minnesota's McKnight Distinguished Artist Award and was included on Oprah Winfrey's 2020 list of thirty-one Native American authors to read. She is the author of crime novels *Sinister Graves, Girl Gone Missing,* and *Murder on the Red River* and the children's book *Stitches of Tradition.* She and poet Diego Vazquez received a McKnight Spoken Word Fellowship for their work with incarcerated women in the county jail system.